Straightening My Tie

Peter Langston

ISBN: 978-0-646-93275-0

Published by Six Nines Imagery
www.sixninesimagery.com

Also by the same author

Six Nines (2009) Kardoorair Press ISBN 978-0-908244-79-9

Head Full of Whispers (2012) Six Nines Imagery ISBN 978-0-646-57539 1

Foreword

What came to mind the first time I met Peter was "where did he get that shirt?" I was soon to realise that he didn't just own one but had a whole collection of them; very loud and colourful Hawaiian shirts.

When Peter asked me to write the foreword for his latest book of poetry, of course I was honoured but I did wonder what I could add, given my career has been in the visual arts. Peter and I met when he came into the Tamworth Regional Gallery, where at that time I was the Director. He wanted to know if the gallery would be interested in a collaboration with local poets; the idea being that a piece of poetry would be written in response to an artwork from the collection.

The combination of the written word and the visual imagery breathed life into each of the works selected. It provided audiences with a different perspective and encouraged them to think about the work in new ways. It is incredible how much an experience is enriched when art forms are combined, one illuminating the other and requiring the use of multiple senses. According to Leonardo da Vinci *"Painting is poetry that is seen rather than felt, and poetry is painting that is felt rather than seen."* Whilst this form of collaboration was not a new one, it was the first time that this had been done in Tamworth and it was a great success.

Reading through Peter's poems, I soon discovered another side to this man who wears very loud shirts. The words in these poems moved me, they made me smile, they made me sad and at times I found myself thinking of past experiences and places I had been but most of all, they made me think.

His observation of the everyday is a strong recurring element in his work, especially his poems about people, such as *Edith, Charlie, and Old Pete.* There is a familiarity in these people he talks about and the way Peter gives us an account of a moment in their lives, we feel we know them or have met them before.

The poem *Universal Truths* provides us with a humorous look on what life throws up at us, even when we are desperately trying to do what is considered 'right'. As a parent, I especially love the line – *"I asked the universe to keep my children safe, they moved in".*

A Town Interrupted makes us realise how eager we are to easily engage in 'celebrity status', even if it is just for a very short time.

Like standing before a good work of art, where one is drawn in wanting to know more. The words in Peter's poems linger, inviting us back to re-read, reinterpret or to enjoy once more his insightful look at human nature and share his view of the places we inhabit.

Whilst I may not be a fan of Peter's loud shirts, I do recommend his poetry.

Sandra McMahon,
Director, Weswal Gallery, December 2014 .

Contents

The First Words of a Poem

Warmth is falling from skies, decadently blue,
murmuring a welcome to an old friend,
thought lost to indoors and symptoms:
to the worst of dark imaginings.
Smiles in the cafe and nods from regulars
who had missed him, asking soft questions,
leaving his corner waiting for him to fill again,
scanning the paper or joined with a book.
A nook outside offers a vitamin D platform.
A bowl offers quinoa salad.
A mug of mocha offers more than the rest.
The end of soliloquy.
The first words of a poem.

He Sings

He sings the songs
which make me
hold my breath.
Waiting
for what comes next.
Knowing it.
Scared to hear it again.
Lips blue,
brain screaming
for oxygen,
for forgiveness.

Uttered.
I'm bleeding meaning,
crying my experience.
Sick I made it his.
Temples herald the pounding.
I fill my lungs
again and again
hoping for protection.
Running my index finger
under each eye's rim,
treading water in my emotions.

Looking up.
Daring myself into contact,
as last lyrics offer sweets,
salve to the pain in all of us ...
... 'till they clap and comment,
sitting in the dark, safe
with someone to talk to,
someone's hand to squeeze.
He, alone, splashing in the white pool.
It's then his eyes come seeking
and smile.

.

The Victoria Hotel

It's raining in Rutherglen this morning
soft kissing the tin-roofed verandah
outside our window.
Little secrets about our love affair
being whispered here and there
between smiles and approval.
The Victoria holds its lover's stories
seeped into her bones
on hot summer harvest nights.
Disguises cast to the wooden boards
as promises were made and kept
either side of lace veils over open windows.
In the Sunday night stillness
a last toast to time
before we penned our chapter.

and the rain
and the roof
smiled
as if,
we were the first.

Charlie

Old Charlie sat in country sunshine,
his town hat pulled right down
to offer his squint some relief
from his mournful, perpetual frown.

His hands, once steady on leather reins,
shook gently on either thigh
and he stole borrowed smoke as the young went past
another pleasure his doctor denied.

He chatted with the words he had left,
spare ... and with pauses between.
Stories once lived and often retold
of the places and people he'd seen.

He was selling tickets when I walked past,
just killing some time in his town.
"Money for kids with the cancer" he said,
took coins with hands creased and brown.

I asked enough questions to draw a response,
reluctant but steady enough
and his eyes met mine, all fire and blue,
"some of us mate, have it tough".

Charlie had joined before Tojo weighed in,
had been with the 19th on Crete.
Had hid from the Hun when the battles were lost:
returned to the farm in retreat.

A hearty young lass soon caught his eye,
along the hard wooden pews he would stare.
Long walks holding hands and the eventual kiss
till it ended with rice in their hair.

His war-broken soul was reborn and alive
he grinned proud at her fast growing girth
and it might have stayed so, as he held his new son,
if his wife had not died during birth.

Ten hard years, in house and in yard
raising a sickly young child.
For the boy was pale, from his first breath,
too soft, too ill and too mild.

It was cancer they said, that bought on the end
and withered the boy from his mark.
So Charlie made another dirt mound,
by the tree with her name in the bark.

He held on to the farm, as neighbours gave way,
outlasting the floods, droughts and banks.
Till a fall from horse, broke his old back
and he sold it for a feedlot to Yanks.

Leaning a bit, he gives his chin a soft rub,
brings his story to a shrugged close.
His eyes are drifting over old times,
to other days, better days, I suppose.

I thanked him politely for sharing his tale,
dropped some coins into his poke.
He nodded and said "here's your tickets mate."
"No thanks"
I was a winner from the first time he spoke.

The Beach

I hate the beach.
The gritty grains.
The white grease.
Having to squint.
No coffee, but
lots of people
to make me feel inadequate
with their sun stained bodies,
hardly hidden,
by patches
and strings
and skin disclosures
young boys go to the internet for.
As I moan the need to worship
at my beach girl's altar,
imagine if poetry
was the great Aussie icon.
Do you fancy
standing
in a room
of red wine stained poets?

Shopping

Standing outside,
leg sore from chasing specials
and shuffling feet
in dens of frenzied female.
Politely avoiding snippets of bra strap
or panties reversed through curtains,
in preparation for the retail lie.
Answering as only love can,
her bum never looks as big
as her eyes are wide
and screaming for ownership.

We walk on,
she with purpose,
me through misguided love,
as if tomorrow
she'll join me at the football.
We follow the navigation signs,
SPECIAL
SALE
50% OFF,
CLOSING DOWN,
seeking Valhalla.

She tries it on.
I chit chat hours,
shop-assisted by smiles,
agreement,
and polite condescension.
My presence an oddity
subject of undeserved credit
as the semi-naked gush admiration
and consensus
over bum sizes.

"Pin or sign?'

Sunshine In The Provence

Sunshine in the Provence
warming my morning
heralding sweat in the fields
as olive and grape
smile flavours yet to come.
Dancing along chains of melodies
from poets and songwriters,
Dylan numbs me,
burns me,
punishes my small beliefs
with his own giant landscape.
Crying for Hollis Brown.

I miss my bed and remote controls.
My country is too far away.
No eucalypts with summer blossoms.
No where to hide in the shade.
I just see the strange and beautiful,
understand only words,
not sentences,
but everyone will buy a smile
from a generous man.

Still,
that first night in France:
happy on the Left Bank
sipping wine
eating what I couldn't pronounce
jet lagged
swimming in the language
the culture
in your little girl wonder,
reminding me I was here to learn.

It's a simple twist of fate.
The Provence fills me
with blithe mornings,
with opportunities not found
on a South Dakota farm.

Home can stay where it is.

Edith

I rarely feel old
A symptom of an enthusiastic spirit.
I find reds in pink,
ultramarine in blue,
hope in despair,
gold in silver linings.

This dull day in France,
sharing uncomfortable seats
on the track to England,
your soft brown curls,
deep, sad eyes
and matt red lips,
your face against the window,
teases me twice;
France, in soft focus,
rushes past,
backlighting your wistfulness.

Your gaze brushes past me
as Piaf murmurs rumours of you
Quand il me prend dans ses bras
Il me parle tout bas
Je vois la vie en rose

I have outlived angst,
purchased a happy life
in currencies different from most,
experiences whose tales I will tell
as sage and time
spice my seasons.
Three decades of love,
more now than then,
despite the same embrace;
knowing *her rhythms*
accepting *her rhymes* ...

... but watching you
I yearn for younger days
when I might have caught your eye.
As I rust,
used and forgotten,
I'll pretend you might have noticed.

Stone Cottages

When the spuds turned black in '45
the O'Sullivans were the first to leave us
their bodies crying life
as hungry mouths tasted the blight
but ate it regardless.
Mary and John and six chiselers.
The little ones never to know
falling in love
or thirst for the Guinness
or laughing with old friends.
No one passed their stone cottage.
No need to go visiting,
the dead live somewhere else.

Daid took loans to survive:
a loan of Murphy's goat,
a loan of O'Donnell's corn ...
stealin' from neighbours
but crying little ones turn a man
when love tests honesty.
The Garda warned him off,
saved him from the ship,
on account of being a good man
when good men
hard men
sobbed hungry in their cold beds,
sushin' their babies
and squeezing their wife's skinny hand.

We were hungry by '47
while they rested black in soily beds,
rotten and lazy.
Oul wan gathered food
from the harder places
in handfuls not sacks.
With too many mouths on death row
they begged tickets
and Shamus and I left
weeping
promises that would never see home,

this stone cottage,
again,
going instead to no green fields
or stories
or laughter.
Still weeping
when news came later,
much later
of no home to come home to.
Our stone cottage was empty of souls,
full of waifs
who died with bone stretched skin
weakness bringing the long sleep
of famine.
Rich memories
sent to poverty
and lonely ghosts
in stone cottages.

Yet fat men grew fatter.
Peeling their bells for service
behind frosted glass
to hide stone cottages.
As Ireland died,
they shot deer,
played games,
talked their greatness;
wove patterns in small pretentious circles,
daubed watercolours of landscapes
with no stone cottages.

Rich men cried for lost privilege
Shamus and I,
cried over the priest's letter
hands bleeding, backs broken,
for torn hearts
rent from us
by the disrespect
so easily offered to working people.
They lost their house,
we lost our heritage.
Only the stone cottages remember now,
their stones rumbling with unease

at their cold memories.

Ireland starves from banker's blight,
come to kill the Celtic Tiger.
Lies fashioned of avarice,
rich men still seeking favour
to boast of entitlement.
Ireland's young evacuate,
again.
Piles of stone cottages remain,
stone by infected stone,
as deep black draughts
write sad endings
to an Irish joke.
The Dail,
in the watchtower,
leaves the light on
but
ignores old stories.

Who will talk of stone cottages now?

.

Know

No
is the answer to
coffee?
feeling okay?
give me a call?
can I get you anything?
will you be joining us?
how about a beer?
did you make an appointment?
RUOK?
are you thinking of killing yourself?

Yes
is the answer to
is it depression?

I gave the right answers:
I guess you asked the wrong question.

At The Gorge

A magpie sings a taunt above me
closer to the passing images
of pussy cats
and puppy dogs
which shape shift as I watch
or return to being clouds.

She calls to a child
and they both descend,
intent on our discards.
Their perches dance above:
swirling ladies embraced
by breezy paramours.

Daylight dawdles,
happy to make the stars wait
while I drink it's unemptied cup.
Greens haze into deeper hues
and a kangaroo ignores my gaze
this late afternoon at the gorge.

Colours

Red

wine

Yellow

flames

Blue

stories

Pink

cheeks

Red

embers

Black

night

White

stars

Green

envy

Red

wine

Old Pete

Old Pete sat looking at the surf
his face, creases of sunshine and shadow
those blue eyes eased now
by crashing waves
and sand
and little kids
and sand buckets
and eagles soaring over headlands.
Blues eyes singed by death and devils.

They had talked over red wine.
Shared their blackness,
hers still fresh
still unanswered.
His, committed to a past he would visit,
not re-live.
She looked for solutions among the coasters.
Now, sunrise behind them,
baking slowly in the sun,
it was someone else's nightmare.

"What's the secret?"
she repeated,
this time without red wine confidence.
This time with nowhere to run,
as though one simple sentence
could be the panacea of all mental torment,
as though his recovery
granted guru status.

"No secrets" murmured Pete,
those blue eyes fixed on a looping eagle.
"Secrets are snares -
and the truth
no matter how unwanted
really will bring the freedom
to find that moment
when self-obsession
becomes self-awareness."

He stood,
walked till the warm Pacific
kissed his toes,
till the first salty drop fell.
Left her puzzled
depressed
wondering,
so far away from his first, wet plunge,
so far behind.

Universal Truths (Song of Samantha)

I asked the universe
to lift me up when I'm anxious:
I got stuck in an elevator on the 29th floor

I asked the universe
to show me what my accountant was up to:
the summons arrived this morning.

I asked the universe
to send me a sex bomb for company:
George Michael arrived.

I asked the universe
to keep my children safe:
they moved in.

I asked the universe
to stop my dog barking:
the cat died.

I asked the universe
why it's omnipotence
included sardonic irony.

Oh well.
At least
it never asks anything,
of me.

Mendacity

She came past smiling
smiling a secret
into smugness.

I smiled back
which dropped her guard
revealed her day.

Head down
she moved to the aisles
to their mundane camouflage.

How could I be so reckless
my big, fresh inked handprint
on her freshly Christ-stained heart.

Wandering my frown
its melancholy burden
avoiding happy faces

forced to shop
instead of
smiling.

The Marriage Wrecking Device

The batteries are flat,
the damn things need changing,
so she leaves her device
for my rearranging.
It sits in the kitchen
where we prepare food
exhausted from use
mocking and rude.

Its the same every night,
a usurping routine,
she goes off to bed
but before she can dream
she settles under blankets
ready for fun
grabs her device
and switches it on.

I've been left for dead,
since she found her new toy.
I can't sleep when its going,
it makes too much noise.
Left to her own de-vice,
alone in our bed.
Giggling and cooing ...
it's not why we wed.

It's not that its new
or the latest design.
She told me "my mother
used to have one just like mine."
Its got a short handle
and knobs on the side
and a long silver bit
that you can easily hide.

She's become quite addicted
to these late nights upstairs
whilst I sit resentful
watching Lateline's affairs.
She even tells friends
things that she's learned,
about self and others
as the batteries she's burned.

Can't beat 'em, so join'em.
Going to chuck in the towel.
Stop fighting her addiction
and go join her now.
I get there: it's too late
She's already started.
The train of restraint
has already departed.

She's added headphones
to partition her bliss.
(It was not what I expected
from equipment like this.)
She's smiling her pleasure
and I still feel annoyed,
that she's plugged into her tranny
with Tony Delroy.

Justified

I didn't feel like mowing the lawn.

I fixed the brushcutter
and did the edges,
trimmed the overhanging trees
and pruned the rose bushes
(yeah, I know, should have done them in May).
I pulled weeds
from the front garden beds,
lots of them,
swept the paths

and after lunch,
I solved third world debt,
fixed the gender divide,
resolved all international tensions,
bought all parties to agreement along the Murray-Darling
and finally proved that Shakespeare WAS the author.

So
I'll mow the lawn
tomorrow.

PS
I exaggerated.
I didn't sweep the paths.

The Meaning of Easter

The Easter Bunny
plump and lazy
leaning against our gate
last night,
dazed,
ears drooped for
all the world a
forlorn picture.
Chocolate smeared his
muzzle, one egg
magically following
another from
paw to jaw,
happy to discuss the
depression he wore with
obvious discontent.

No, he had not
peaked early, or
been fooled by an
errant iPhone calendar.
A fit of mania hadn't
put his arrival forward. This
was no bipolar bunny.
No.

Wary of competition from
the church he
had resigned his
role on the eve of
his big day.
When department stores sell
chocolate Christs on the Cross
even mythical creatures have
had their day.

Much The Same

Much the same.
That's how I've been for weeks
when asked
by worried adults
who look like my children
grown up.
I can see their fear,
hear their unasked questions,
my longevity
suddenly questioned
in things unsaid
and said,
time no longer healing.

Much the same
repeated to friends
used to my frivolous comment
fallen absent
online
in cafes.
Counting the folds of skin,
once smooth
and rosy.
Waving instead of
feared conversations.

Much the same,
these weeks
of losing weight,
stomach cramps,
nausea,
hair loss,
worry,
regret,
anger.

Much the same,
looking at her,
thinking who we've been,
what we've survived,
only to slide away
in small bits,
so stealthily
she doesn't realise
she's losing me.
Won't let me talk of it,
only some alternative
that entertains a future.
Yet love for her
eats at me,
much the same
as it always has.

For Dann

I thought of you today
as sunshine played peek-a-boo
with running clouds
Of stumbles and falls
and faltering steps
bloodied nose
and overdose
still rising
rising to step
to stride
to run

I thought of conversations
through tears
of history
of desperation
at useless medication
and relationships tattered
by misunderstanding
and fear.

I thought of your spark
a pilot light still burning
midst the confusion.
The creation of
words and pictures
of evocation
inspiration
conflagration
where light met dark

I thought of your struggle
with sleep
with black dogs
with sexuality
with a furtive mind
with truth
and how to tell it

I thought of trust
offered to me at your worst
born of hope
that someone else knew
someone else cared
someone else could offer
real shoulders to cry on
without fear of stains

I thought of courage
rebirth
sunrises
and the millions
of new thoughts
you'll know
you'll share
you'll pay forward
when it's your turn to listen
to offer connection

I thought of you today
and smiled

Poppy's Paddock

Standing among the sugar beet
as soft rain confuses autumn sunshine,
I can hear them screaming
in this French farmer's field
on the rolling Santerre plain.
Maschinengewehr rattle away,
cranking death or worse,
bullets traced on a starless canvas,
finding flesh and bone to rent.
Slow turns take it all in:
maps and diaries and body tallies,
no longer point and click accounts
or pages turned for reference.
I can smell the earth.
It sticks to my boot tread,
wedges beneath finger nails,
pancakes on my knee
as I crouch to touch it,
to make the connection
between this place
and home.

He's lying out there in the dark,
in a land for no man
full of fallen men,
this dying half kilometre of red dirt
to Monument Farm.
He is only stories to me,
told by my mother,
of my father's father
and an old scanned photograph,
larrikin grin,
baggy suit,
fedora pushed back,
eyes sparkling trouble, even in sepia.

A farmer waves recognition,
one grandson to another,
steering his harvester through sugar beet,
working soil bought with obscene riches.
Standing in the fresh tilled field,
I'm close enough
to cross the gap of time,
to gather the experience
in small parcels standing in the crossfire.
Long terrible minutes of tears
tear their own damage,
as I cry in loud sounds
and confusion.

I see him finally,
opened from one hip
to the other nipple,
lying for six hours in the mud,
refusing to die,
his mates changed
into corpses
or walking carcases,
the emotion hollowed from them,
replaced by steel
tempering their survival,
only to rust at home.
No telegrams for their families,
just a slow vacancy
of lunacy and grog.

I'm trapped in a conflict,
pacifist disgust confirmed,
family pride overflowing.
Nothing to offer
but tears I can't stop.
I found the grandfather I never knew,
lay his medals among the sods
to be soaked in his reality.
Bridged a connection to his son,
walked on the bones of conundrum.

The field of screaming ghosts remains,
just south of Villers-Bretonneux.
Southern Sons calling from the tilled rise
across the Hangard Road,
their voices low and tired,
groaning since that 4th Anzac.
I placated them with tales of Pop,
news from four generations
after their rough run
to Monument Farm.
I cried with their remnant memories,
scattered among sugar beets,
shook with disbelief
we could be so cold and cruel
over a point of view.

I offered gratitude inadequate,
spoke the Lords Prayer,
left them there,
another callous re-enactment.
My face washed clean,
I'll keep the deeper stains
as ammunition against hawks
with swooping points of view.

Madness Hangover

I wake with a madness hangover,
vulnerable only in dreams.

Outside,

other universe shift workers
hum the starshine,
numbed by the safety of talk back,
their cars screaming obscenities.

Feckless children do adult's work,
prying openings from windows,
seeking keyless entry from doors,
snatching their living inshadows.

Drunks walk conversations past
in anger or tears or laughter,
all shouts and whispers
and loud conspiracies.

Inside,

I touch your forearm,
waiting there on quilted overlay.
One tingling square centimetre,
enough antidote to madness.

I take my gameface
back down into sleep.
The zombies are outside,
moaning like wisps of wind.

Noisy Neighbours

The people upstairs have been dancing all night
The noise of their music making me quite uptight
Thumping and bumping above my bed's ceiling
Singing along with volume and feeling
Partying the dark hours
Constant drums peeling.

The bloke next door has just started singing
a repeated loud chorus from his throat is springing
he's perched on a fence post and oh, what a hoot
not only sings like Domingo but in a fine dinner suit
Singing at first light
and now with mates in cahoot.

Then with sun, came creaking and groaning
and an occasional loud crack to accompany the moaning.
The sounds of old men, moving bones out of bed
Rust stiffened joints and the complaints that they said.
Walls winced their age,
floors complained with each tread.

The stairs scream a herald above the soft whisper
of a near empty kettle in air that is crisper
than when the last meal was fed to the fire
Breakfast is swallowed in flaming desire
and laughter roars up the chimney
at winter's attire.

I'm exhausted from sounds happening around me
The rain on the roof and magpies who sing carefree
An old wooden building stretching with dawning
The fire downstairs, crackling and yawning.
Accepting my place
in an Aussie bush morning.

Explorers

By Strathfield
someone's Nan
was teaching me Sudoku,
insisting Japanese minds
imagined these French squares.

Before Hornsby
the first complaint
when another Nan (they're everywhere),
wished for perfect past journeys;
and condemned all things modern.

Before Gosford
the conditioned air
was too cold
was too warm
was better than being outside.

By Wyong
the ice, ice babies
were swearing their threats,
demanding hot chips,
having beer refused.

Before Broadmeadow,
the ice men cometh.
One felled by lost-headed men
compelled to use violence to reject it;
the other engaged in cubby hole cowering.

At Maitland,
visitors in uniforms
applied pepper spray
when words and reason
proved foreign.

After lunch,
all complaints suddenly resolved,
all meals agreed perfect,
we settled down to read
and Sudoku.

Tempest

You giggled,
a deep, guttural, naughty girl sound
stopping to mango-smile as
Yasi howled for blood or
at least the roof.
Sitting in our rainwater reserve,
mango juice running drip lines to
your breast,
one drip suspended waiting for
company at your nipple before
splashing in diffusion in
the water circling your waste.
Tin groaned above, its
ceiling diaphragm breathing the cyclone,
in and out, as
you sucked the stone for
last soft mouthfuls of flesh.
Extending your arm to my lap, the
stone was discarded with a
soft thwap on Lino
wet from displacement and
writhing bodies drunk
on wine and sweat and fear.
Your hand found strawberries cuddled
in a wet tea towel on
my bare lap and
choosing one, traced my midline to
a hungry, breathless mouth,
allowing my tongue a promise and
then withdrew to your own rapacious lips.

Something large broke outside and
shuddered the wall I slid down to
a new, wet Lino seat,.
My chin bought forward to
the rounded bath edge, a
hard resting place to
watch your disregard and
count the peach stones
stacked at your clavicle.
The candle light,
perfect incandescence for feast residue:
broken biscuits, red cheese rinds, banana skins and
fallen grapes bobbing in tomorrow's drinking water.
Noticing remnants of fruit amid the sweat and
seeping temptation from chin to waterline, you
retrieved your glass, recently refilled and
loosed it at your skin, submerging softly with a wink,
your breasts floating among the debris of
cherry stalks and pips and a spreading red wine slick.
A dog howled in unison with the wind and
we howled for a moon we imagined.
Wicked contempt painted your lips,
shone from your dark eyes,
no storm your master.

Four Gneiss Girls

Girls pass,
decorating Peel St
in their various stages of decline,
maturity jettisoned by desire.
Craving womanhood
via wrong options.
Tits pushed up and out
to be noticed,
scowling if you do,
dirtying my old manness,
accusing me
before I can think it.
Costello kids gather on corners,
their mothers missing English,
permanently,
to he-said, she-said
their days in skinny tops
and burdened jeans.
Death burns between fingers
and spite replaces spittle.
Sex has burgled their childhood,
chained freedom to a pram.
No time to giggle boy-stories
with friends
or share lip stick.
Whilst the Impies crowd rages,
there'll be no thrill of seduction
in between feeds at Mum's house.
Here on street corners,
dressed like tarts on the public payroll,
the generation gap has stretch marks,
yellow teeth,
a narrow vocabulary and
a tenuous grasp over financial planning.
"I was readin', right
or watchin' on the telly,
that it costs 200 fouzand bucks
to like get this little bugger to 18.
The friggin' govment is only given' me 5!"
Like the Yarra
the gene pool flows upside down
in the Lucky Cuntree.

How Many Times Have I Told Ya?

Don't give any cheek when you're on the bus
How many times have I told ya?
Don't leave your bike at the top of the drive
How many times have I told ya?
Don't throw you uniform down on the floor
How many times have I told ya?
Tidy your bedroom before we have tea
How many times have I told ya?
Finish your homework and *then go to bed*
How many times have I told ya?
Brush your teeth and then off to school
How many times have I told ya?
Don't hit other kids in the lunch break
How many times have I told ya?

The bus driver said what?
Your bike is where?
You can't find your uniform?
The bedroom's a mess?
Your homework's not finished?
There's grot in your teeth?
You got in a fight?

What do you mean I didn't tell ya!!!!!!!

A Note From Jessica

Something unusual happened this afternoon
As the sun drenched me
and the most patient breeze
played with papers which rule me,
instead of adding columns
and hefting the heavy parts
of the decisions others waited for ...
I thought of you
and smiles burst from me
like caged birds released,
startled by their freedom.
In the stillness beside the river,
roaring with the silence of small bush birds
and a sneaky goanna breaking twigs below,
I broke the silence with a laugh you gave me
as wild things watched on.
You said laughter and love were candles
used to light other candles
shining as bright after sharing
but with more to share the task
of keeping the dark at bay.
I haven't smiled for a long time,
can't remember the previous laugh.

I guess we forgot important things
as the details flood the vacancies life creates,
the holes punched in a day
when the doctor talks of dark masses.
Holes that rip and tear and end your universe.
Each damn breath has seemed a mountain
since I kissed your cold lips that last time
and started shuffling papers for salvation.
Sparrows scrambled for crumbs at my feet,
crumbs from those cakes I said I wouldn't eat
and their persistence bought you back
suddenly
vividly
beside me laughing at my bald head
just revealed and shaved in sympathy.
You returned to me laughing,
your eyes sneaking blazing blue
between the crinkled slits of your mirth
as you rocked back and forth
roaring me to strength with your laugh.
Yellow in the sunshine
I smiled until sunset,
my heart glorious from the memory
of your generous soul.

Sans Voix

Yesterday:
harsh words
spoken hastily,
ribbon cutting moments
long after construction toil.
Your attack,
earned by others,
fell on me instead.
No eggshells left,
I walked to avoid chasms,
rubble raining down.
A quiet afternoon,
all pretence it never happened,
till tension snapped before sleep
and the second wave.

Today:
an apology,
heavy with qualification,
conditions,
excuses.
Blame
always proportioned.
My share
explained to me,
responsibility implied
with a laden trowel.
It all feels so familiar.

Tomorrow:
sore and tired,
home and easy temptation
will find me scapegoats
I am learning to ignore.

Listening

I can see you're
scared
of what's stopped
hiding
in the cracks of
stories
never told by
you.
Love is in the
air
thick with anger
confused
by apparent healing and
time
spent happy it was
over.
Righteous anger without
guilt.
This is your story
too.
Tell it your
way.
This time I'm
listening.

Discoveries

Dead houses
doing their silent, ghostly business,
drowning years gone by
when life sap-surged their veins.
Silhouettes in silver
under a million million lights.

Called to life at first hues
by new tenants
white and pink and duck brown
suntanned orange in that first hour,
life in every room
and toes dancing in their cool bath.

... and I can only watch
and wonder
and listen to their stories
wafted to the shore by zephyrs
tip toeing over gently pushed waves
and breath them in to my safe keeping.

Between Suns

1:00
Coughing
Reading repeat sentences
repeat sentences
while the house groans

2:00
Coughing
The cornice crack
smiles at my discontent
as I count patterns
on wallpaper,
on the same ceiling
catalogued last night
Cat coitus
disturbs dogs
One slipper
cold foot
colder tiles
hot tea

3:00
Coughing
Valium

6:00
Coughing
Blue running down to orange
through tree silhouettes;
Chill creeping past my dressing gown;
Stevie Ray and Sheryl in my headphones;
Both hands around her ceramic mug;
"It's six am and I'm alone"
sitting in my own noisy world;
Something to write about ...

So Easy To Forget

Sunshine on the Clarence
makes haze in the late afternoon
when summer dresses for Christmas.
Grafton runs down Prince Street,
stops at the Crown Hotel
to watch the Big River roll past.
Dead men are rightly honoured
in the small park,
bricks gates and stone walls
memorial to their sacrifice,
to their loss.
Heads still lower on Anzac Day,
"they shall not grow old ..."

In a corner
closest to the wharf,
a small pointed obelisk
stands and watches,
forever trapped
in a December afternoon
of absent men and wartime:
watching little boys sink
and their mothers,
running down Prince Street,
wailing at the shore.
Whilst Grafton's men died elsewhere,
thirteen small figures
died at home,
sank to the mud in leather shoes
and back packs heavy with memories
and treasures
gathered through their laughter
and a day on Susan Island.

Nine of them lie safe,
up in South Grafton with the kangaroos,
high above the flooded waterline,
heart break etched on stone in gold letters.
Four in town are not so lucky,
dishevelled and broken.

In Memorial Park,
the glorious dead are rightly venerated,
even by instruction,
"Lest We Forget" ...
... whilst a small pointed obelisk,
no bigger than an eight year old,
stands watching the Clarence,
the names on its faces
so faded they can't be read,
little names so easy to forget.

Bobby, John, Graeme, Billy,
Brian, Dale, Sono, Toby, Ray,
Bobby, Keith, Cec and Eddie
Lest We Forget

Pierrot

A sad day
when a fairy dies
Drowning not waving
An escape plan
devoid of choices
Ending pain
beginning woe
Black water
I once gargled
swallowed
till clapping hands found me
their light glistening my tears
under the surface
Ready to leave
needing to leave
but saved
to sprinkle fairy dust
Fairies are crying tonight
sparkle dulled
by the nine o'clock news
Clap your hands
hard
please

Sunday Mornings

Sunday mornings,
once hot sex and laughing,
now ritualised control,
regulating the next week
into little bundles of chemicals.
Snapping plastic lids on joined boxes,
so assassins can lay in waiting
to ambush me,
reduce me
to social acceptance.
I am safe.
They are safe.

I miss the wild ride.

The Time Thief

In the car
afterwards,
you spoke of the oppression of fascists;
Hitler's black stain on humanity,
a legacy enabled in the since
by other pox stained sociopaths;
cold Death touting for companions,
in endless whimsy,
in clouds and empty streets.
Death,
a euphemism of creative fence sitters
too intelligent to believe in God or the Devil
but too scared not too.
You cried their deaths again
standing in the rubble of the book thief,
all blue eyes and golden ringlets.
You marked disbelief
at seventy years a Jewish Hollywood
had never told of Germans suburbs,
terrified from the air, from within.
You crowed pride at homegrown wordsmiths
and a local tradesman,
hammering each word into place.
Passion dripped from cut places
wounded by a story well told,
infecting heart and soul.

In the car
afterwards,
I listened
and wondered who'd won the cricket.

Walking

Walking
Sunshine and Fidler
flooding me.
Left my life
where I tied
my shoelaces,
content to stalk
sad words
and laughter,
warmth and a soft breeze
while someone else
cries.
No notifications
No status updates
just the chance
to stem the tide
ignore its roar
its demand
To place the world
in stasis
and hear
only my own breathing
and the sound
of lost compliments
Walking

Beholders

I saw you before your smile
weakened all the men,
broke every woman's spirit,
in this very public room.
Your façade,
teeth dominating
between broad full lips
drawing the light,
the energy,
from every other personality
watching you with turned heads.
Your green eyes
twinkle, twinkle little stars;
high cheeks and swept back hair
accessories after the fact;
heels clicking authority
like feline jackboots
as you move among us,
taking it all in.
Taking us all in.
Men shiver teenage dreams
the memory of sweet, sweaty nights,
guilty mornings.
Women gasp scorn
turning whispers around corners
past pearled earlobes.

Still you hide in plain sight
untouchable,
wanting touch
wanting frowns
disapproval
tears
reality.

I've seen you before your smile,
lurking in shadows,
desperate
for coffee
for old clothes
for garden dirt
under broken fingernails.
Before your smile
it sulks there
screaming for help
pleading for escape ...

until another door
opens onto lights,
adulation
pedestals
and you smile.

Town Interrupted

Delight,
imagined,
at near things.

Last week,
I almost drove through Werris Creek.
Almost saw the spot
where she might have stood,
gazing
distracted,
possibly by a brown dog.
Just a brown dog,
kelpie maybe,
but brown
and pretty much
a mongrel.
Impressed,
she moved on,
most likely,
with a famous gelato
and takeaway cappuccino,
renamed in her honour.

Angelina moments,
large in small lives,
recorded in newsprint
with the fluency of cultural cringe
and nothing else to say.

Train whistles drowned
by wolf whistles.

In Werris Creek,
even a brown dog
is memorabilia,
at twenty bucks a turd.

That's probably what happened.

To think,
I missed it.

Killing Justin Beiber

Perched on her lonely battlement stool
the songbird chirps of sweet and sour
stories of loves lost
gained;
of hearts broken
mended by second chance
of tears tracking pain
down faces tired from the game
of Linda on the radio.
Each song ends
warmed by their generosity.

Requests are made
and met
with smiles and gratitude
as though they were
her universe.
They reward her tonight
service a debt
unaware of ungrateful nights
of competing poker machines
football screens
and ten beer heroes.

Tonight
the dingy pubs
the six straight gig sore throats
the calloused chord weary fingers
the midnight miles to home
the practice, practice, practice
the hard yards along the country mile
the art vs the pay cheque
the day jobs for petrol money:
tonight
three hours balance the ledger.

As hard case kisses guitar
a ten year old says hello
immersed in her music,
her smile, her wink
and acclaims the songbird his idol
sending Justin Beiber into eclipse
and Sally-Anne to top his pops.
Such sweet critique
even from starry eyes:
a reason to sing again,
tomorrow night.

Cote d'Azure

On Sunday in Monte Carlo
the sun sheens my arms
pushing droplets along the hairs
like milked spider venom
even at half seven.
The beautiful people,
perfectly perfumed,
perfectly dressed
to the right
where their indulgent excess
rests in five star comfort.
Rubbing shoulders with themselves
Cloning about on the Riviera.
Even their farts are designer.

Down along the Boulevard Princess Grace,
plebs, interlopers and poets
gawk at the view
overcome by the Cote d'Azure
and the distance from home.
Breasts are released,
freed of Nanette Lepore
with new Ferrari fanfare,
homage paid to Dr Fisher's
plastastic fun bags.
Lauding le révolution chirurgicale
as though it would save the third world ...
whatever that is.

Up at the Casino
when the chips are down
small countries are bought and sold,
large ones held for ransom
in moments of whimsy ...
... while a dairy farmer's daughter
yearns their experience,
stars in her eyes
with a ten Euro stake.

I watch all from breakfast
sipping tea ordered in French
"Bonjour. Thé noir se il vous plait"
cobbled together in days,
said as much to impress me
as my hosts.
The Mediterranean smiles its seduction
as I write these hypocritic oaths

Blues Country

Blues man singing to an empty room
weepin' of life in harmonic sevenths
and words that sting
across this voided space
like winced reminders
to open long closed lids.

Outside
big hats pass
heeled boots dangling below the brims
leather belts holding thumbs
as signs of life, search for country
and a babe to buck.

At the pub (all of them)
men with "eh" post-stitched to every sentence
scream suggestions to the willing
who have pushed up jingles
to jangle with ever back beat,
exciting every achy, breaky heart.

Back at the blues café
the harmonica is crying.
It's the witching hour
and narratives remind me of my loves
and too many failures.
The blues man sweats my blood …

Just me and some of my best memories
tapping our feet,
thankful some passion still flows,
some art still holds to its responsibility
and custodians still spit up life
through blood-soaked brushstrokes.

Neil Young At The Rose and Willow

I'm lost in beyond the blue imagining
as the sun lingers on this early winter's day.
Soon to leave for someone else's summer
it warms this small, north facing lunch.

comes a time, when you settle down

A southerly stiffens and wails past the corner down pipe,
looking to be mischievous,
a premonition of it's July misery.

comes a light, feel it liftin'

Thought spills pumpkin soup in my beard,
my mind distracted from nature's ceiling
to Neil's own clear blue sky thinking.

you and I were captured, we took our souls and flew away

Fat yellow rose heads nod appreciation,
unmolested by passers-by for table decorations
and gasping this last sunshine.

comes a time

A willy-wagtail chats me from the lawn,
hopping closer to make his point.

oh this old world spins around, comes a time

By the time I sip my tea and make plans till sunset,
I feel caressed, placed at safe distance from myself.
Rose and Willow has begun my transformation

comes a time

A Simple Twerk of Fate

Bus stop
(rain)
Conversations about
rain
Fears of
hail
"because of what it done
to me bruvez ute
last time"
(thunder)
"O my G" one gasps,
only partially de-abbreviating
to prove her individuality,
to give the impression
of rising above
the condemnation of birth.
Her friend,
content with the universally applicable,
strangles a whispered *"faaark"*.
Moments pass
quickly
and pass on to
stolen conversations,
with Angelina at the IGA.
Angelina in Werris Creek.
Sightings and near misses and
how brave she is
and
(thunder)
grabbing both breasts
"they couldn't have mine".

Silence at the bus stop
defeated quickly by
a sister's all night sex story
excusing a yawn;
(rain barks and meows)
"Mylie Syrus is a slut ...
... I used to like her too";
bashings, grog, coppers.
(flash, boom)
"Jeeezuus"
freezes them,
freezes him,
trapped on either end
of social bipolarity.
Silence at the bus stop.

Miming his disbelief
unseen
in an alternate universe
of white leads
internalising Dylan,
it was then he felt alone.
(thunder)
Satisfying his disbelief
by emphasis.
(hail)
stings his arm in transition
from bench to bus.
The only passenger leaving.
Leaving the chit chat abandoned.
Leaving the rain outside.
Leaving him ashamed to escape,
to retreat into his middle class bubble
unchallenged on an empty bus;
whilst ancestors develop lung cancer
accompanied by idle gossip,
without acknowledging his departure.
Silence on the bus stop.

The driver,
lonely for a smile,
accepts an iPod stare
and watches him in reverse
plonking ungraciously
ten rows back.
Speakers
over modulating,
overcompensating,
for Mr Sullen.
Screaming reminders.

Mylie Syrus
slut-singing him
through the suburbs.
He wished he had not gone straight
but he accepted
a simple twerk of fate.

Little Things

I lost you to the little things:
little things you expected,
little things I didn't say,
little looks, little sighs,
little things that went unnoticed.
Little things so hard to explain
as you were leaving,
your bag packed with little things
bulging behind a long, sad zipper.
Each little tooth biting a farewell
in unwilling collaboration
to forever hold such little things.
Little tears from your eyes,
little buckets filling mine.
This great love reduced to simmer
by other lusts
as money or position or accolade
ran their fingers through our hair.
Little remnants and complacency
sharing kisses behind our back.
Unfaithfulness often needs no lover.

The mid-morning taxi swallows you,
the driver's bit part a detached portrayal.
Your head down behind his glass
your chest heaving sobs
reserved for the dead
at funerals.
My one last, little wave
a final hopeful act,
several hundred acts too late.

Autumn closes around me,
changing colours
and the restless dryness
sweeps about my feet
condemning me by the collectiveness
of little changes
and little things.

I Gave You Flowers

The hibiscus waved apologies
whilst bees and hummingbirds dropped in
to tell more natural truths.
The Brisbane air was heavy
with sweat
anticipation
fear
but we smiled through reception.
You laughed when I pulled face
sand mocked your gown.
We normalised the day,
convinced a dark mass was shadow,
technical failure,
anomaly.

Melbourne was chilly
even in April sunshine .
I stole flowers from hospital gardeners,
roses and carnations
arranged them on your bed.
Your beanie swum about,
no hair left to anchor it.
Routines were setting in.
I could still make vomiting fun
but sang Paul Kelly songs
when the mirth escaped us.
Memories came and went
so I talked our life and
we held hands against the world.

New York was noisy and hot
even for a Queensland winter.
Cab drivers asked about holidays
as you swayed into Huntington.
I alternated viburnums with black-eyes susans
for you to hold through bad news.
Hydrangeas in Vienna,
red geraniums in Paris,
delphiniums in London.
Sydney lavender crushed in your pillow slip
placed in secret
as you buttered tears across your fear.
The last of Charlie Teo's cuts
made in despair and waste.

It was a quiet welcome in Bowen.
Women hugged love into me.
Men squeezed my hand in hard silence
their shuffling feet finding nowhere to look,
jaws grinding and swallowing lost words.
Their emptied pockets,
shocked into silence
still ready to help.
I wanted to tie yellow ribbons,
jealous of the oak that embraced you.
Your smile had become yellow hibiscus.
Later, rain scrubbed at my laugh lines.
I looked for you by the boats on the beach,
tried to remember when I had bought you flowers.

Untitled

I tried forgetting You.
You came back.

I tried forgiving You.
You wouldn't accept it.

I tried writing about You.
You got the message.

I tried speaking to You.
You snuck off.

I tried telling the world about You.
You made me hurt,

again.

I tried not to dream about You.
You woke me, crying.

I'll try to sleep,
exhausted,
tomorrow.
You won't let me.

I try explaining the depression.
It never works.

I try not to see the blood,
You spread,
everywhere,
every time
I close my eyes.

Not Today

Not today
when reds blush vermilion
and bacon invades my air
with salt and fat,
the blue sky out-deeps the sea.
Every noise clear and captured,
even disapproving sighs from old ladies
projecting judgment across a cafe
filled with chat and unhappy children.

Not today
when my shirt,
deliberately loud for such a day,
disagrees with the mirth assassins,
as does my insolence
and laughter
and intensity.

Not today.
as I smile past your disapproval.
In a day of parades
crowds applauded,
my 76 trombones.

Not today,
as ideas cascade
waiting in uneasy queues

Not today.
Come back to tomorrow
when mania hides again,
when normal will be alleged.
When my eyes are dull,
my spirit flat,
when I'll have no brains at all.
Take you chances then,
but not today.

Someone's Daughter

Someone's daughter **died** last night
'cause someone's son came home
Someone's father cried 'till light
His wife just cried alone.

Someone' brother **beat** his wife
for lonely coffees with his friend.
Her sister says she'll make it through
but the next fist may be the end.

Someone's mate **raped** his girl
and beat bruises in her bones
he left her in a foetal curl
discarded and alone.

Someone **held** my daughter down
assaulted at her front door
Attacked her like her husband had
as though she asked for more.

Someone talks up promised days
of gender equality
When our daughters won't be men's **slaves**
but it's not the reality.

Someone said the monster's gone
but he hides inside our screening
Till he can weakly justify
handing out a **beating**

Someone talks a politician's **lie**
but promises come too late
Tomorrow restraint will not apply ...
... our women **are not safe**.

The Cheshire Cat

I saw you this morning
as I turned from stoking life into black logs.
The birds were singing the sunrise
in the Blackwoods by the noiseless river,
which crept past again last night.
My feet, bare and fresh from bed,
numbed by cold old floorboards,
rubbed heat from the sanctuary
of a loungeroom rug,
as first crackles laughed from the fire.

There you were,
on screen saver duty,
acting the Cheshire Cat
in a rich man's garden,
as fountains frolicked
in syncopated madness
to Tchaikovsky and Bach.
From Brushgrove to Cape Ferrat,
with that same smile,
that same heart,
those same twinkling eyes
which imagined wonders
long before seeing them.

My five second treat vanished,
supplanted by three small children,
in a poor man's garden,
wearing little more than their mothers smile,
hair wet from the garden sprinkler,
posing for some future embarrassment.
Poor to the point
that Fruit Tingles on their pillow
were a treat beyond excitement,
cares not their currency.

I remember gasps in those gardens,
thirty years apart.
My arm squeezed for support
as though her legs might buckle,
or swoon overtake her dreams
becoming realities
in a rich man's garden
and watching the spark she had started,
in our own.
Both gardens so full of treasures
that only the Cheshire Cat
could have imagined to life.

Catching The Bus Home

Standing audience for a hundred sails,
the northeast offers fair winds to aid their zigzag journeys.
I stood beneath Bradfield's magic steel totem
whose power has drawn strangers to a country
brave enough to imagine it.

My own imagining sees proud men here,
watching strange figures in stranger skins,
as blackfellas drop before pointed thunder sticks
after raising spears and yells.
Yandu -ndhu balubuni -l-girri nginya balubuwayi-l-girri
(If you kill you must be killed)

I flagged a bus which promised me Australia,
in this journey from wet heart to dry suburbs.
The seats offered thin relief up George St.
From front to back, all seats gave the same ride.
Smooth was smooth, rough was even rougher.

At Flinders Street Station, Ariadne Gianopolous (ari-ad-knee ... gee-an-op-olus)
sat heavily in her seat, a tired figure in black.
Black shawl, black dress and a back stooped with life,
she bore treats from the city for Apollo ...
god that he was to his grandchildren.

At Constitution Dock, Wang Wei stepped lively,
running from the hot oil of the China Diner,
from the Peking Duck and No.47's of his father
to the arms of grandchildren who miss her too,
but first, greeting us graciously before seating his thoughts.

Aanya Yadav (an-ya ... yad-av) flagged us down along the North Terrace,
quickly settling to the rhythm of avoided conversation.
Laptop in place, she adjusted meeting schedules,
checked her stocks and tweaked a presentation,
caste(ing) off the constraints of her mother's role.

Abrahem & Jacoline Steyn joined us carefully at the Swan Bells.
She, flushed with colour and full of baby,
discomfort persuaded into hiding by camouflage smiles.
He, full of worry and lost in the love only 26 can bring.
Aircraft design and equations were for other days.

Such freedoms were a long way from Camp Aguinaldo,
When the bus pulled away from Douglas Springs,
Marvin Quicho was dripping pools onto the floor.
strapped then in a disgraced uniform waiting for Aquino.
Blue skies and sunshine heal old men too.

The Story Bridge sparkled in the heavy air of early evening.
Emma and Joshua heaved their packs onto the bus,
each brimmed with Kiwi wool and bits of the Lonely Planet.
They laughed at us through clipped vowels,
beaming when we met them with sheepish rejoinder.

Nguyen and Tanaz flagged us down amid leafy round-a-bouts,
offering passengers gratitude and guilt in equal measure.
Tortured at home, tortured here and tortured in between,
they talk of late lectures and part time jobs
and parents who will not understand.

Aboard the bus "Australia" we become used to each other.
We share packed lunches and language,
talk of who we are and who we might like to be.
Behind us, the past is many things we can't change
but ahead lay choices left for us to imagine, to enact.

In Cronulla, we make one more pickup.
Youths tear the destination sign from the bus front,
cape it on board, like bullet-proof supermen
staggering from seat to seat to spit in our faces.
From fear, we all rise in anger ...

... until we realise there is no driver.
The only way to our destination,
the only way to find "Australia"
comes with the same tolerance of years
that kept us happy in our seats as we travelled.

We invite them to take a seat,
settling in for some more rough circle work
before we venture back to the open road.
We'll get used to each other
in the miles before we change.

My Dreaming Place

There's a moon over the Murrumbidgee tonight.
Silver reflections dancing on the ceiling
as the wind ripples the surface,
trying to shake off the glare.
Night birds are calling.
Kangaroos, restless from daytime heat,
move about my campsite
looking for marsupial junk food.
Little noises of comfort and familiarity
beside a bush river.
Nestled warm under feathers,
the steady rhythm
of her breathing
beside me.

Just woke screaming a change of meds.
Scared,
not by what's finished,
but by what's still to come.
Dreams I chased away before,
taunting me to shut my eyes,
to come and play in their backyard.
Outside in the moonlight
things seem brighter,
simpler,
colder,
inviting.
In my dreaming places,
I'm still not safe.

Running Away To Sea

I can smell the stranded weed, rotting
where last night's tide abandoned it in
careless piles to decompose
in the slow spring sun.

Waves brush at the edges, drawing
strands of mermaids hair hopeful of
resurrection and rebirth in
the bosom of this blue day.

An infant breeze brings tidings of
cold places, less charitable.
Friendless bitter places, wet
with regret and siren's promises.

The bumpy, white roofed horizon stares
back at me, staring back at it, full
of daring and mockery of
my pretence of greater sorrow.

I have not been to ride white caps,
tempted a sailor's fate or
smelled pirate blood on a rapier wit,
sheathed and blunt on this blue day.

Back in the cafe, no solace, no
safe corner to read, to escape from
the idle conversation of a lonely woman,
an abandoned weed seeking her own redemption.

So to this bench, by the shore, in
the feeble sun, too weak to shield me from
the child of ocean blows to come, but a
refugee wrapped in words none the less.

At The End Of The Tar

East of Narrandera, at the end of the tar
the locals are leaving, such as late afternoons are.
They've spent most of the day, dragged behind boats
and wave at the night folk arriving to dote
on the wide Murrumbidgee, still wandering far
past new chums, just passing, the end of the tar.

The river turns millpond, at the end of the tar
as the kookas start calling and noisy galahs
swoop from dead trees to reflections complete
as wood ducks make bow waves like small naval fleets.
A white cockatoo's claxon the late quiet does mar
for the folks on the bank, at the end of the tar.

All talking has stopped, at the end of the tar
save for little nude urchins splashing hoorah
Feeding nature their freedom, their laughter and cries
while their parents sit pondering what will become of their lives.
But for now, it's all wonder. They are who they are.
They don't understand, they're at the end of the tar.

A soft breeze is stirring, at the end of the tar
The herald of rain, when the south wind blows hard.
It sharpens the senses and changes the scene.
Dark grey in the sky makes leaves vivid green.
A storm is approaching, the clouds give a bark,
as all creatures find shelter, at the end of the tar.

Straightening My Tie
(Cover Poem)

I'm tiring,
thinking it would be better
not to think
I'm the only one
shouting to be heard
full face
eyes bulging
into the latest gale.
Standing on the line
ready to meet injustice
with metaphor.
Writing wrongs.

But
there are other things to do:
Becauses
becoming
B-causes.

This morning
I woke up older.
Still with passion
and fire to achieve.
Still with time to spend

but on myself.

I'm tiring thinking it would be better
not to think
I'm the only one
into the latest gale
shouting to be heard
full face eyes bulging

Standing on the line ready to meet injustice with metaphor. Writing. wrongs.

But there are other things to do; be causes have become

B-causes

This morning
I woke up older
Still with passion
and fire to achieve

with time to spend

but on myself

79

Poets Notes

(page 1) A down day ... went to my favourite café (Café 2340) ... wrote my way out of it

(page 2) Written for my son, Chris. We have a special relationship which can be as simple as meeting eyes when he is performing.

(page 3) An old hotel Sue and I stayed in at Rutherglen, near the Murray. It had a romantic feel ad I imagined on past temporary residents

(page 4) A true story, re-told after I met this old bloke on the street in Inverell selling raffle tickets for kids with cancer. Cost me $2 for his amazing story.

(page 6) We go to Yamba every July - have done for more than twenty years. Love the town but hate the beach.

(page 8) Travelling on a bus to Aix-en-Provence, homesick and listening to Bob Dylan. It reflects my adjustment to being so far away from my comfort zones.

(page 9) On the fast train from Paris to London I sat opposite a young woman who looked like she had been cast for the role of the typical French country girl. I called her Edith as a homage.

(page 10) In the one day at Killarney, we visited all that remains of a village of stone cottages. These were abandoned during the potato famine in the mid 1800's, when a third of Ireland died in their rural homes after sending their young men to New York and other places for work and survival. This was juxtaposed with a visit to a rich man's mansion, who had invested his life's fortune in a visit by Queen Victoria, hoping it would buy him a knighthood, lands and further wealth. Bertie died a week after the visit and the rich man was forgotten. The last part of the poem relates that to the crash of the Celtic Tiger in the last few years causing young Irish to be emigrating again.

(page 13) It can be very frustrating answering honestly when someone asks how I am going. There is the truth and then there's the answer they would prefer.

(page 14) Sitting on a bench watching magpies at the end of the day at Apsley Gorge.

(page 15) I shouldn't write when I'm drinking.

page 16) Fictional. The idea struck me when I saw an old, weather beaten bloke sitting on the beach watching the waves and a much younger woman beside him, talking constantly.

(page 18) Call me a sceptic but ... written after someone tried to colour my aura.

(page 19) Just a girl I smiled at in Woolworths. I got to thinking about the face we put on in public.

(page 20) I love reading this poem at gigs. Always creates a lot of giggles and then a sigh of relief at the end. The idea came from a misunderstanding when talking about flat batteries with a mate.

(page 22) Sue left me a list of jobs to do around the house. I wrote instead.

(page 23) I saw chocolate Christs advertised online by a church in one of the states of southern USA. The one thought - "that will put the Easter Bunny out of business" - spawned this poem.

(page 24) Another one of those public face ideas. I used to be honest about how I was feeling but these days, it easier for others if I'm not.

(page 26) Written for a friend. I've watched her struggle. Proud of her progress.

(page 28) Proud of this one. Written partly in France, partly when I came back to Australia. My grandfather was wounded at Villers-Bretoneaux in 1918 and Dad had always wanted to visit the place but work and children and an aging wife meant it never happened. I never met my grandfather but I did Dad's trip for him, placing his medals in the dirt of the paddock he was shot in.

(page 32) A Nundle poem. A couple of times a year, I stay at Nundle for a week to write.

Written one morning when I was suppose to be editing. It was raining and the day was just starting.

(page 33) A true story of a ride home from Sydney on the Explorer train. Two guys, high on ice, went nuts on the train, when the a staff members ask them to calm down. They were taken off the train and we all watched through the windows, horrified, as the police had no choice but to draw weapons and capsicum spray them.

(page 34) Fiction. I liked the idea of lustful tempest of the female central character while Cyclone Yasi roared outside. This is about lust and abandonment.

(page 38) I had wanted to write a poem about the Costello babies and their mothers for a long time. I was going for more empathy than I achieved but a walk down the street will find these girls easily enough. Gneiss is a volcanic rock formed from other rocks. The girls in the story look like girls but have been hardened by their experience and loss of childhood. This is a companion piece to an earlier poem, "For Nice Girls" from the Six Nines collection.

(page 38) Jessica Rees from Southern California died in May 2012 after a ten month battle with brain cancer. There are two remarkable elements to her story. Firstly, she spent all of her moments from diagnosis to death, blogging and using social media to raise awareness about brain tumours and to encourage others who were similarly stricken. She signed everything she wrote with NGU for "never give up". The other remarkable element ... she was only 12 when she lost her fight.

(page 40) Written as a reaction to a few tough years Sue had with menopause. A bit brutal I guess but never the less I think I'm expressing some level of understanding while I lick my wounds.

(page 41) The compendium poem to Sans Voix.

(page 42) Camped beside a small, shallow lake which was full of mostly dead red gums. I was up early - sunrises have a special place in my recovery - and watched the place wake up.

(page 43) An I can't sleep poem.

(page 44) 13 little boys drowned in the Clarence in 1943. The names could hardly be read on the memorial stone which is placed in the corner of a war memorial park in Grafton, about 400m from where they drowned as their mothers watched from the bank. In 2013, I was invited to read the poem at the 70th anniversary, where new plaques were unveiled.

(page 46) Written for Robyn Williams. Pierrot is a character from Commedia dell'Arte ... the sad clown

(page 47) Every Sunday morning I sit on the end of the bed and set out my pills for the week.. Reflecting here on gains and losses.

(page 48) We went to see the Book Thief, which largely unimpressed but I pay homage to it before revealing my preoccupation on that night.

(page 49) Probably more a strategy than a poem, this is what I do to maintain some mental balance.

(page 50) Fiction. Saw a women walk into Cafe 2340, perfectly manicured and polished. Her PA ordered for her. I wondered what was behind the mask.

(page 52) A reaction to the media crap that dominated the local paper and even local ABC radio when Angelina Jollie was filming locally. I thought Whitlam and Keating had killed the cultural cringe.

(page 53)True story, retold to me by Sally-Ann Whitten the day after a gig in Armidale, of an adoring 8 year old fan approaching her after the gig and saying he liked her more than Justin Beiber.

(page 54) Literally written in the breakfast bar of the Hotel Fairmont, Monte Carlo one morning as Sue slept in. The have nots in Monaco only have $5 million yatchs.

(page 56) Written for Guy Katchel. Four of us were his only audience when he returned to Tamworth for the first time in years to play at the 2013 Festival. Armed with original material which was politically edgy and licked with blues, he played his heart out while cowboys went past on their way to pubs and country rock.

(page 57) R&W is where I stay at Nundle. I was listening to Neil Young and taking in my surroundings.

(page 58) True story of an afternoon thunderstorm, waiting for a bus in Kable Ave and the ride home by myself. Myri Syrus had just done the Springsteen cover. Juxtaposing lots of Dylan references with the musical integrity of modern music and my middle class existence with my working class roots.

(page 61) Fictional. The story of a relationship break up.

(page 62) An extrapolation of the true story of a bloke I know who bought his wife flowers every day while she was in the final stages of dying from cancer. I exaggerated it to show their desperation to find a cure by fictionally adding travelling the world. The flowers mentioned are favourites of those cities.

(page 64) Open to mean whatever hurts people the most. For me, its a personification of the evil that was done to me when I was 11.

(page 65) I have written a fair bit about being depressed. Set out to show the flip side ... the mania.

(page 67) I get very distressed about violence directed at women. I chose to rhyme this one so that the words would be anticipated and therefore have more impact. The bold words emphasise the violence.

(page 68) Not many poems in this collection about Sue. A Nundle poem. Spied her on the screen saver, looking like the Cheshire Cat, in the gardens of the Villa Rothchild in the south of France. The next shot on the screen saver was a photo of the three kids from the mid 1980's, dressed in undies after playing under the sprinkler. She had always put so much into being a mother. Both treasured memories.

(page 70) I grew up in the Sutherland Shire, so the Cronulla riots were in some ways a shock, yet in others, the culmination of a middle class racism which has existed there since the 1950's. I am asking for us to embrace multiculturalism in Australia. A giant, continuous metaphor, using place names from major cities and the dominant ethnic groups which had emigrated there. The last three verses marry it all together by asking for us to even embrace racists.

(page 72) I was taken to the bush before I went to school and have always gone back there to find peace. This was written one night beside the Murrumbidgee, with all its delights, after waking terrified by dreams caused by a change in medication. It could equally be a metaphor for the sudden and unexpected discovery of danger in any place of refuge.

(page 73) Written after withdrawing to the refuge of a park bench behind the beach at Victor Harbor. Minutes earlier, I had found a quiet back corner of a café to sit and read, warding off anxiety, when I was chatted up by a lonely woman looking for "someone to hold me in the night".

(page 74) A little bush poem inspired by a quiet camping spot beside Bundidgerry Creek, a local spot for water sports east of Narrandera. The only other campers were a couple with two small children.

(page 75) The title poem. Picks up the concept of Eric Bogle's "Tired". I had the line "Becauses becoming B-causes" floating around in my head for years. Passionate advocacy can wear you out. The title comes from a line I wrote in a play, where I described writing as "giving my mind a chance to straighten its tie".

www.ingramcontent.com/pod-product-compliance
Lightning Source LLC
Chambersburg PA
CBHW050557280326
41933CB00011B/1874